T0128494

# This Love Affair

A N N E T T E   S T O V A L L

**author**HOUSE®

*AuthorHouse*™
*1663 Liberty Drive*
*Bloomington, IN 47403*
*www.authorhouse.com*
*Phone: 1 (800) 839-8640*

*Published by AuthorHouse 06/29/2020*

*ISBN: 978-1-7283-6003-4 (sc)*
*ISBN: 978-1-7283-6002-7 (e)*

*Library of Congress Control Number: 2020907588*

*Print information available on the last page.*

*This book is printed on acid-free paper.*

# Contents

## No Finer Love

Even as oft he'd embrace nothing wrong
nor ignore commitment to more of her love induce,
would none say nil to admiring ideal
that, here, at last they with the rank ideal admired for
lovely roost yields.
Nor jubilance recites of rank if Love going wrong
from where each day delight surrounds home.
He's glad the house where view the wave in ripples
where a scene at coast so near
and seen the back yard fruit tree would no fruit cease to grow.
How could he ask for more.
Only that who more valuable than hue in printed stripe dress
and lips elastic than the painted red roses bloom
should not leave, nor he from her beside rooms
where seen is that of visions night.
Especial like the Love of whom he loves.
And where this lake to running bluest wet waves to wet ridge
of nude joy to arc,
It looms above the valley dark,
It rouses twilight summer's lark
where better hope is of surpassing fear,
even as only he would pleasure her who near.

# The Splendor That Blooms

It bares the blooming will grow as if tunes
from soothing music night and day call
by add the melody to rouse it all
when ecstasy eves like the splendor with noon.

It blooms and blooms till trumpet notes wane
if winter cues the august notes would fail
when eager lips and arms grow cold and pale.
But warm designing makes for bloom again.

It blooms like rosebud tall below skies.
It cheats Taurus to be akin to Paradise.

# The Love She Wanted

Now, this one looked until she found him.
She knew for her he was the one by
the way he walked, he talked and flashed smiling
his fair smile best along his fashion shirt style.
Everything about him for starters then
said he was the one to win.

So, they wed after dated 2 years.
Had 3 children best she given birth
and trendy caste for upgrades home they here.
Every other moment close, they giving worth
to seen they holding hands they caress.
And where baked on flower sparks on blooming best.

No one has doubt that yard with oak tree trunk
beside the bunch on hedges evergreen
how fencing yard around the yard at fashioned best
every caste wanted. And where two most seen
of kinfolk and friends would never to ask
how they seem, for now, 2 achieving Love seems best with
more they refining how a best Love should be.

## My Time With Love

Days in better memories call
were the golden days and nights we appraised love.
They call me back to early moments along decade.
Fresh the garden fields to circle upon spring
when much on county soil for had cohesive things
we loving like the little frame home of we drawn to then.
Came 5 o'clock my call in "Awake dear"
was ever drawn to love for dutiful this husband young.
His duty for the work he came and left from,
I send him off how delicate brand at arch door where
the bliss he needed of my own signature style kiss
while 6 o'clock round clock still ticks.
Comes 7 o'clock with cardinal pigment scarlet reds
around blue jay beaks circle chirping rated main
for chant my 27 years to woke again.
For now gives cause to I arouse beloved 3 who
the young be sons abide around daughter.
"Awake my 3 loves, and let the baby sleep.
School is not yet it rounding on closing
Make haste my pretty ones.
Time, never it slumbers."

## The Better Years

In the summer of our life,
then were the better years.
Then evenings we alone we loved more
when life was good with youth years.

We laughed where we held hands
beside the stalks in grass yards loom
for we knew most we were beloved.
Adored when summer song birds croon.

Everything we did was fun.
Even in summer and soon autumn rife.
We pondered not of what may ageing steal.
For these were the better years of life.

# Short of Something

This is no unreal as rare buffoonery
that it lacks room enough and bends imagination rune
to dreaming of where the choice winds main to run
and where the humming birds won't dread to hum.
This too short of space with won't increase of chair styles
enough for who else lives how inordinately abides the while
talk this husband to convey words enough in house
he times addressed her sweet on fortitude hurts.
She's shy and sweet temperament different from her mother.
Why do not your hurt want you reply back to me your hurt
if sad or otherwise comes up.
If I indeed afford house upgraded roof class enough,
then come away with me my sweet
where nevermore to hear of or see
a summer of just day baked too warm,
a dragonfly pitch appears glum,
a glad public speaker's ridiculing heard,
and plane too near for strike hit the broad raven.
And maybe then we'll stay the love always.

# The May The Moon Resides Beside

Must you go kill the good of tepid weather.
I wish you back to May rayed our day
When tame heat branded all who around her.
And premiere love so mildly dressed in May.
I shall not wait but track when you back glad
With more the free birds humming passerines' hum.
You love to mutate manners from what had.
But moon to guarding eve it stares out from,
Awards a twist may turn from how gets mean
This now is cold these days have cold is untame
For some black cloaks in drab the altered seam.
Oh moon, how spring in May makes recurrent claim.

Come trek with me beloved amid assess
How so like May a time will switch the dress.

## When Love Is Good

When searched in town had more the red birds there,
How long relations and I searched as could!
For kind should know attraction too sets mood.
We keep the sight on ideal to wed fair
And later on the butterflies glide in air.
Such they are fully graceful to behold.
The man we seek in favor young or youth old,
Yet will we love this more his kindness lay bare.

If someone would be perfect, much for doubt.
The worthy gentleness ranks for what should.
It ranks who fared around stout fence about.
Glad I was when the comfort he gave me good.
Love flounders when passed away fair good is not.
Though glad he may somewhere he wished he would.

# I Love You She Loves Hear Said

"I love you," he said.
Words I love hear and proud
how "Love you," said over.
Whether be gleam or sere winds clouding chief words flow
when bliss this while I hear beside
would none do for set eardrum bend the stiff ear.
"I love you," she's discerning this while for here beside.
Whether if summer suns advantage on house between high trees near
or if frost chills the dark ledges chill dew.
Were I to doubt everything you raised spoke words the fair as
choice gems incite the core of me,
my life 'neath raised roof edge for becloud plank rooms fee.
"I love you," he says here again.
Whether act on this we lose or win,
we share the love we stall make.
Whether kind or best for sinning
of the will is unwilling.

## The Big Question

### A Man's Question

Pretty woman, adorable ideal of my dreams
your beauty is alike to limbs to circle growth in fair blooms
upon June tree in season.
And tenderness real as the tender grapes grow ripe soon
on hue on baked on vines.
Pretty one adorable, could you be the love desired
for be mine?

### A Woman's Question

Pretty man handsome, attractive
and gentle as the sweat upon the spread with summertime tree
and the way winds flexible blowing on spring.
Pretty one, handsome and gentle arms out-stretch to me
could you be key for be mine?

### Another Man and Woman Hopeful

A gentle one, adorable and character how sworn
to best ideal in mate I dream of, even longing for my own
will I ever find one?

## True Confession

The leaves are falling, falling, dropping
the foliage spreading on stretched out sidewalks crop.
How many days I think of you!
You are also lovely and shoulders broad!

The cones are falling, falling, dropping
redolent pine scents on squirrels and nutmeats out.
He came to my door night was late.
My hand dropped like lavender oil
sweated fragrance by the hallway. Late
the hours were such no guest should call.

The fruits are falling, falling, dropping
even pulp sweetness on the ground yard too props
where flowers fragment their autumn prints.
If I'm the woman you to seek day and night,
you even could say to me,
I want you near by my side, stay delight.
You are a flower and like a tree
whose fruit will be sweet of my night.
You even could say that to me.
The way we of now, only owing to bit contentment
soon or late we will meet again.

## Confident About His Promise

What if Neptune became like red earth Mars
and folk became more like Nemesis for.
If violets none for bluest sapphire hue but pink instead,
and if the painted rose most only red.

If now saw fruit on orchards even bear
the mixed-in fruits which a tree never dared
and wine hues lavender grapes that once suitable
now a twist of bunch dim coagulated specks into.
No matter how they altered fashion these yields
no matter how suddenly they become
except for what another fate would allow
I doubt if altered interruptions how
would keep me from home here duty and love allowed best.

### If Love To Last

Where you find Love in city, town or suburb,
if Love to last, it must grow on true Love.

# I Like Her in Red

I like her in peppery red looks hot.
Don't get me wrong.
I like her frame in dress blue, black, green lime too,
and clad waist in rustic dingy pants tone.
But shade attire if red denotes her looks ravishing in salsa tone.
How comely she strolls peppery red dress at jubilant acts zone
that domicile walls line.
She perks up gloomy looks mood mine from forever long keep.
When times she wears her hot shade heels, they go fine
with saucy hot design frock I won't fast lay sleep to snooze
when tendency of mine about admire she struts hot,
indoors or somewhere out.
If you ask me, primarily, she loving hot the salsa primary hue
because I man her mate one loves the red primary too.

## Then And Now

How loved those days I doted on evening while
We shared embrace beneath the still sky clear.
We touched beside glad spring with serving style
The slack yard crowning rose the house had near.
We nodded at who cruising lane when what some
Nodded back glee as mine for love seeming grand.
Slow ran our day we wanted not become
The love marks chills like nipping buds at hand.
And now that oak tree swells upon the blue bird,
Our tree a mark for love though spring with skies
Appear this gross to some who raised a harsh word.
While youth designing on what for day to rise.

Come back a better love if leaving someday.
Although comes lift in have the love you stay.

## A Pleasant Surprize

A certain package no disguise
Of looks as outter attractive size
As one for having Love's choice prize
Between the tucked fast lace adorns the rounded insides
Is no miff.

And if in polished wrapper ink dark
Of worded print marks the ink dot mark,
Or medley if sweet pebbles circle a sweet spark
On the pound fill for one in mind,
Such comes from who handed it to this one who still
For him who handed by affection of will
Handing it to her one still bestowed lovely inside.

# A Poem in Spring

Life we spend serving time, I looked by a hall threshold
Where draft to serving April fanning town's metropolis.
If I could learn to love you more, your change mood
Lets me show you how.

I gift to you the solid hue red rose
My affidavit greets you here;
For since your sharp temper placates me enthused
With alteration turns next endearing mood.

I will to you a seemly treasure true
Beside the sparrows twitter carouse
With straddle municipal lavender lilies pollen.
We spoke chats like gems for the incoming hours.

How could I not love you better?
My oath heaps the summer blood in your cheeks that I
Even would small shy from,
From I could learn to love you better sum
Than dust spiking April month will go from.

## Summer Amenity

There was a time the amenity fashioned
the brighter sky it baked proof
that decades ago had no more better proof to see
than it rayed the green and fresh grass and trees
ran more for keep sore defiling air from long keep,
a thing of ours we reap.
So much the trend today of sore marriages fail
that I long for true love to keep.

And the longer I resided at far county town
breathes air where local sparrows hug around town,
would much my desire at night I longed for such time
to be with who more would air his smile
he attracts me near to him all for keep to more
he'll see me again in rooms the blue gray sky above.

# Romance the Main Ingredient

I love you, miss you.
Recall gets far beyond miss you.
Did not we verify agree to cruising class blended with scene
we walked and talked at heat on grassland seen.
And nigh to flash ground flora budded summer flash seemed
how ornate seeming lilies hailed whatever justly we had.
Did not we praise how dining out gave sentimental ties thrill.
She had her answer pat frank he said back,
"We held for dance hall you appraised. Our hushed affection too
we dined if when beside the rock ground boardwalk prop.
We traveled, shared the go enroute to uncover scenes plot."
I love you, miss you, I'm crushed, her reply.
Sere days, sad her joy hurts how flat endearment sered out.
Why could theirs not have been main
the sweet romance should blossom privacy same
as a sweet woman wants it romance uncovered from due.
I love you, miss you.

# For A Late Chick

Listen up Chick. The amenity dies while I'm in room
beside the hall for swift return.
A duty investigator
should bail this one husband out right away
from how this house with an acute slate.
It builds permission for likely me soap enough
and buff the floors and not forget I bake and cook up
some nights the main feed.
Now here you come with greet me in the hall late fare
like late you are too often the wife from there
the crowd acquiesce to local bar fare.
Unlock these inside tasks. Straighten up!
The way the workload goes it's hard to see ever
how the 2 of us yet we drawn to each other.
But tired for have, since we yet drawn, more leeway
some fix could specify what one on one talk does me
would fix the roster straight out straight.
That some lay cause to kids—cause may be.
Our kids are wee and quick to clamor with play.
Resolve I won't fault if undermines bar clamor—that's love,
just as much as when one's on time is love.
Here wields time for what a man to mate I tell again.
It gives concern to sick about how much love
for bar habit leaves you less for here, too, kids with me,
since how you greatly rated rates main for be late.
It leaves me no surefire love from who a late Chick.

## I Cherish Love

I walk to know a pleasing vision rhyme
How glistens the route like shafts from above.
I prize the shelf in trees like jades in rhinestone.
But this most of all, I cherish love.
So few relations from here city so fair
Like few more waves engendered more waves rest.
So well I see the silvery evening where
I gaze how bright, still, the avenue east and west.
But this most of all else, I cherish love.
The shadows veiling climb the hill they of
Till I no longer learn what hills uncover.
I see the gloom that starry eyes commenced of,
And know then, if not all love hails from above.
And this most of all, I cherish love.

## Too Long to Date

Was she the piano needed play,
or tame as barbie dolls on holidays?
She had her doubts but more sure
this time her truth had met arch link to strategizing lure
to draw her out of house the many long hours the trap
she trapped in had her inside with intense handicap.
Sure, they became friends even dated sums on her chest add up.
All had her hopeful of behind 12 years long running,
no right surrender but unto the vows worth marriage.
But Oh, she was just wrong. How could he not care?
Was she a darn doll, a piano,
a fool, a puppet on the string like sums
he dangled extending her malcontent?
And no right excuse he proffered her amid the lack had his par
for nothing trip to the altar's arch
he'd exhilarate her with wedding ring's diamond.
Past the breakup, it left her to wonder sums up.
Why should he date someone he did not care to want.
She cared right enough.
If she was a fool, she still is a dim wit dunce or she's
the smarter fool who likely knows what she wants.

## A Father in Love with Home and Family

His arms are filled with gear.
Toolbox nails for panelboard a room,
two cans of vivid latex paint for a second room
rate for he starts remake makes good with garb a home.
And child in right grant for the grounds around
the low grid rail of railings upgrade fence,
be child each their bliss happy at play in yard then
with toys between the grass less weeds around.
This dad who blends in with group for same,
same right unit who gets him happy about be with them.
He makes time with time out like here
for chore duties, too, his expedience suits him.
He tacked the last panel he raised late in evidence ranked
real as a raised floor plank.
He's tall short, and tall is running short on perfect build.
Ideal is for who mate is ideal
she even grins to hear it mentioned even
of his name.

## Sad Habit with Pipe Dream

They love they dwell beside the stream in view
allows fewer sparrows disturb daydreams roam
since do exist.
Nor do sprawl grounds all disturb who with short porch
behind bulk loading of calm hedges thread miniature bough.
Spring the Peaceful scene.
And comes on hesitation
this parting of the ways half starts at realm zone.
On more occasions they brawl and quieter ways have some
dwell with 2 who must part with bitterness ways.
And zone is near at cement hard on half the board walk when
construction sets a purlin roof in town is how
delivers how more the brad in transit.
And nearby way a county stream half is not far.

## The Mood Ran

It runs again of some city
wherein it even too with mood runs
for town with virus it worst suns
the bones in with fever pitch.

I was in this mood pitching heat
the ardor ran just how on fellow
acclaim I had for him went well
till too well he lied to me.

Then heat in me went crowding sly sway
I tried for crowd inside my chest.
But it just then invitationed guest
arrived my warmth torrid sway.

It swayed to net it saddened looms
till added there my heat less bold
off ignite mood to chap it cold.
Like spring cooled the hedge mushrooms.

## What If

What if blaze sun more for halo less bright
entered the main event but not without light
how moonbeams between how shining still
did nothing more than stay the rays moonbeams fill.
I yet remember day we first met went well.
The spark in you left me thought of nothing else.

If nothing blame to name ambience weather
how spring comes up anointing man with laughter
that we ourselves residing happy with having,
then most would be results have in ideal.
Sorry, I fell asleep last night between yields
you said no blame of how our love comes up more real.

## Sage Comments

For some Love is forever.
Love comes to some people only once.
Love for many folk sums up to more than once.
One date leads to another or departing from.
Dating ranks for finding out what will or won't do.
Show politeness upgrading nothing pretense.
Abuse is not Love.
Get out soon as abuse starts.
Wedding bells rank swell for even seniors.
Love is where you find it but hopefully not indebted
to someone.
If life seems a challenge, it is.
The wicked lover who escaped could one day entrap her tight
around yet again.

Poor people don't always care for finding another someone
to love who's also poor.

You can know if a love is real.

The love that's real does not suddenly wear an ugly costume.

## Amusing Statements

One fed up husband to his wife: Some days I wish
you were a book so I could read what designing big fuss
on your mind.

One man to another: Why do you call your wife
sweetheart a lot?
Man's reply: That's to make her think she is
a sweetheart.

Wife to husband: I wish you would erase that knowing wide
smirk off your face.
Husband: But you know it's never true when I claim
you drink more beer than I do.

One woman to another: There's only one thing my tight
husband nosy about, how much I pay for fancy those tall
spike heel shoes.

Wife to husband: Why do you always look at fashion high class
women on the street?
Husband: It's not what you speculate. I only look around
to see if they notice how good fashion I look.

Wife to mate: You're a banana shake, and I'm a sweet
treat don't fuss. But nobody knows about it but just us.

Woman to another: My husband wants to scream with every-
time I say I paid $400 for trendy stripes itsy bitsy up
and down bikini.

# *Love on the Amends*

I remember vaguely how like an autumn marigold fades,
I strayed fade night from home our love fast fading too,
becoming pale like gravel on the broadout ledge hillside
with little more for we could voice or do, a man said.

Then, suddenly out from you, I realized in the moment
hinted of love not for all gone
that a scale pebbles worth somehow could be worth saving.
And now I'm back behind revealing walls that a man favors have.
And sharing of the rate our better accord allots it rhyme
with each day I'm seeing how home interpolates more defines us.
Such favor certain I am we both want it instills
on our insides award us where pink lavender daffodils,
what we both want more pleasantness. Though, yet, recall
of fade night disorder looming somehow upon the hill.
Thus, we try remember best how love we share still.

# Stay True

I love a lovely day like now, this gal said.
It seems to beckon us where out
we stroll to birdwatch at backwoods heat pine crop.
Unless you rather, that is, to just you go
to where you so loving be with pals just
and I track at grounds heat woodsy scenery just.
What must you amount of that?
I state it better this approach go arm in arm
where stroll agrees to watch arrayed marigolds bloom.
Do that if you rather we do.
Suspicion alarm I of more
perchance you bent on stall.
Since your go time happens more of late
with pals won't shun drink booze in foggy bar
men game for lurk around main for hunt cute chicks.
Do what you please, she said.
But of this much be sure I see
you never to cheat on me.

## Loving How a Profile

Symptomatic of how alike to delicate refrains
where leaf is blown around chirps are fair strains
Symptomatic of how her feet walk.
And shoe fits well if none to fit assails walking.
And better mode gets rumor tongue off disturb
her deeds with fair verb than tweets a fair bird.
Her style in line with trace sobriety nil over,
it only ranks for fame yet in how sobriety sober
as painted on table designing paint where heard her blessing
sometimes a psalm of her said long or off excess.
She takes to arms of him would court her delicate flounces
get mellow or they more pronounced.
Endeared moments, purpose, love too will adoring embrace
around her fame she designs of sweet mace.

## Searching for Love

She went where she hoped to find Love.
To nightclub, liquor bar,
picture show, concert hall.
Oh, she met up with men, some at darkness prime hours
had entered on before some late diversion closed.
At the nightclub she met up with youthful dancer danced
too much, left her tired on feet and butt,
even stepped on her toes.
In the liquor bar she met who drinker drank too much
gulping his beer and bloated mix brew every chance had.
In the picture show she sank teeth more into scrumptious bar candy
than she could even speak to someone.
At the concert hall not much fun.
There most she met fellow not one.
At home on the computer internet, her regret in heaped gaze upon
weird looks man had around bush top for goatee,
no man she wanted see,
like other men those she checked off her love list.
So she now in her thirty's losing hope.
But cheer up honey. I know what you mean.
Odd case will come to this. And other odds even some you may need
could add up to sums other things.

## A Situated Circle of Flowers

A situated circle how
Perimeter blooming bent
On surround and come again glow
Dim rhyming dust from which I went.
When I touched you in slight sunrise
And after early let to morn
For the stride along breaths belong,
I walked at quiet before the storm.

Will I see him torrent evening?
Will I see him smiling fair.
Do less affections let him believing
With storming dusk of night he could mourn
All for the Love in me to treasure?
If again I bring fair pleasure
Still fading glad in me you treasure,
Then, back, I bring like a flower less charm to you.

## *Affection Looks*

It comes to this out seek companion with should you look
where first in where to look is less for be forsook.
Is it search through the mall? In the theatre? Hall is
farfetching
annexed the hall concert hall to when short intermission.
It could be on this paved agrees walk arrangement
his looks of Countenance fair ere it warrants Estrangement.
Sometimes it best at home by the telephone
tells of him blind date forthcoming he shoots for who unknown
while drive at streets he had nil for Estrangement dulls reap.
For truth there is a yen for the best find may last for keep.
If one for set and shoot for looks outlining who
the best gentleman for looks appear gorgeous hunk do,
It helps if linking looks to tag with Courtesy required of who
in touch with Patience, Forethought, Cleverness admired.
It comes a time this awareness amounts true grain
with true a gorgeous Countenance must wane.

## After He Left

Even before the voice could add God's assent,
came howling bawl to rain keen and clear.
And bawl this ritual weeps weeps to less calm since
not even then, did calm settle fear.

At home, each painted room looked bare
and gloom the silence saddened all would accost
her mourning ached the sorrow her care
brought on by him her lead one gone to war.

Now past the gloom, her soothing belonged
it stirred less passion for whom past the need.
The tangent note, they who service or kill
the same who enlisted those vows to heed.

Besides, her move to where scenery
to go with now the man seemed to her most grand.
Just when her feet for tramp at moss the emerald green,
in walked her chief one with suitcase in hand.

Now, would her months gross vows have woes.
At that sure note was she limp as the rose;
and thought, then, to meet beiges bare tile floor.
But came herself to silence door.

## A Lovely Guest

It gifted on late December
I 'bide who tendered me
The sets in such an ivory gem
It libels a foot degree.

It was although my birthday
Gifted for Christmas eve
That I was cued for scanty mirth
In one his knack perceive.

As far as I knew gift morale,
The vestments past I saw
All set for such a knack ivory crystal
Few glims and great I saw.

'Twas once upon December,
This once I was afraid of
'Won't keep to know me,' but, now, I know him
For, next, he damaged love.

## Goody Love Mates

This one is kind who thoughtful
To him begins with goody.
But all is not smoothly, just fair.
An image she generously snooty
When she opts him behind another.
But trusting prowess he won't care,
He takes her back chaste goody.

# Death of a Traitor

Why not straight out and tell me, dear, what you may make
of me those days have reached a point a late moon
may not for settled in on all your hair a hoary white,
nor might you have same grisly skin exhibits wear the same
as I could have of tufts the lines from ear to ear.

What will you think of me when who among those days, dear,
are 6 x decades?
Yet will you love me if perchance I sad for how I may have
then have become.

I say to you by the Book I defy be the cheat.
You swear to me by the Book you defy be the cheat.
We both swear to each other by the Book we shun of even give
a lecher or strumpet stay in the house.

Who played out?

The gardner refused who he is man of maintenance
The speech maker refused who could not type well
The young stag refused forever with short antler;
Brunet is glad she gone from be the mistress.
And who for on the trip to nowhere might lead to somewhere,
who could have starts in Trinidad, tomorrow.

## I'll Admit

From how they hug my hips, I hum the sigh
of somehow regret for how slacks fit my thigh.
These shops I shop too with I'm reflecting comes through
with reflect back on some others mirrowed here too.

Before don the wrinkles dress for his and her tunes,
she felt like wearing it to some other for livingroom
than attend his limitations operetta pitching song
a dismal showing of what comes to harm.

Now, they attend concertos must know hurt hearts.
They will no pain before like shoes they nuzzle partly
squeezing sly manacles till the right lyrical flute tones
they send to each other high notes be like the wind to race me on.
Such the love affair they living with becomes.

Dresses wrinkle, pointed toe shoes defaming fit swell.
Whomever ever I choose to love, he must do suit me well.

## Woods The Way You Are

Look at you! all dressed in common shirt.
No one for common rate hath made you thus
With just enough rare knuckle joints worth
To me in palms we touch.

And crabbed hair so thick weaves in knobby goods
I'd know your caliber weaves trace anywhere
Your trace scented locks like tangled woods do
the rate at colored wrens share.

Don't go pulling back from garbing limbs do
Some turns have other tress diminish wiry scar
From it addresses hairstyles you do
It rates for turns you, next, for.

## Familiar I See

Where caked on ivory blends vogue I meet
These slight on paint blends having caked on grooming,
The grooming they renewing on and should complete
Advancing how autumn frosts the love affair.
It's clear how it only appears unique teems
This love of floss floor ground as to way of movement seen.
And public moves with some have warrants on hearing
If stunted upon ageing has dimmed on hearing;
As if they favor more they follow steering
What ageing moves toward it ageing wise.
And type they favor love when summer appears,
They motion of a style with more they clear
Of summer grooming fair pavement styles near.

## Love She'll Vouch or None

Now, she may promise him, Oh, sweet delight
Born in tangerine straits Gibraltar
Allots this right to him when sot gone straight
Surrounds this glee of hers to offer.
But she'll not vow her mate, Oh, glad glow
If given where around redeeming slight
If mood he'll heap wee sober he'll do
If, then, will undo delight.

## This Love Seemed Right

She felt it was Love just right.
Seeing that he opened with finesse car door just right,
took her to trendy restaurants inclining nice,
bought her stout finesse vodka the quaff bar had right
and bought for her a bit sheen glitter from jewelry store.

With Love blooming right this way, their wedding soon arrived.
All went smooth, desirable swell between first she admired
of the average swell residence how life resided.
Then, one day mate demanding to her hurt,
give up cleavage dresses plus short mini-skirts her happy right
and out at local bars too much, not right.
Demands to which she then agreed to, not enough.
Suddenly came his abuse strict, he dispensing to her sad groans
raw beatings and throat bruising choke downs.
Causing soon she left with all hasty retreat right
that next for ponder where Love veered off passion swept between
one day for life rejuvenating her when on satin sheen clouds,
the next for she was crushed to stiff base floor ground.
This one was better off who did not stay but soon left.
But pity who would stay and lost her last breath.

## Two for the Weakness

Yes, I have flaws unkindly blemish
will be.
Slight odds I'm hooked at West Coastal
days get clear.

And you, my friend, grown familiar
with odds,
have traded pleasant romance
for cloudy day slow gets clear.

## Love on the Hill

"Gal go inspect beside the valley hill
and see where distance not far
if wild bluets dent the grass with rise still."
Dear Mother I'm guessing hot summer with same
it raising sorts uphill much the same
as what we witness to this dale down low.
Unless you fear the swelter could very well maim
the bulk uphill it differs blends.
"True, it could, though bring the mustard blade
I love for spice put season bit swell.
When much your father living, spring days we rose
for we commenced where hill declining stay hot.
Beside where our picnic we sealed there our love
We seasoned bliss how bonded sweet touch.
The buttercups in grass smelled sweet like cloves.
When you go hike the climb best than I could,
bring a few gorgeous wild bred bluets the hand full
along with dandelions tall as rise free.
And main for the love of I value dandelion tea.

# Night with Dark Gems

When a digs where monotony she'd go,
the pane of such it monotones glow.
And something for it frigid frosts glass
sending glow by the room when icy snow this crass
it lots no spawning of green twigs allowed since blocked.
And where at way she loves her mate is not blocked:
his wife about where, next, it remarks of heat
denied them andiron since furnace allowed heat.
She flashed her lip red ink she smiled on dearly walked in,
husband with paper stiff the sheen in rare tin
he placed to free ponderous her rote day slates
if thrill in hand, a box of chocolates.
As soon she kissed who icy cheeks ached cold,
she took of this her swarthy gems gold
'fore passed along to each, now, sample elates
who each tongue craved these ink dipped dates,
mate and 4 children for a deep dark tone mite;
and felt good, then, of somber night.
At dawn, she looked there for caliginous row,
her gems all gone, and I should know.

## Love, Love

Love, Love, Love
who can capture straight Love.
I had a first married Love but hubby died soon.

Another Love flat off reliable that spark so flickered out,
was like the few I met did not stay around long.
Not even one designed for so design proposal that it
would style for hear piano clue the wedding song.
Who was I who traced it averages long years
with habit rooms became trend?
Only the average young woman stern on hope real.
Karma greedy for have both Love and skill,
the years peaked how I morphed into became Poet, Writer, Artist
when yet designing on ecstasy Love included.
Yes, who was I exactly. Was I who just do
for becoming old? Was I too ugly, inept? Was I mean,
the female darkie abusive like some demeanor cruel women
and base those men who choke down sad women?
To say base won't even it style shaming how mean.
Whoever accepting straight Love someone to give,
be thankful even that right Love does exist.

## How to Rate Singlehood

Since namely fair espial
Approaches marriage,
They bound won't shake red
Some cheeks off flush.

Deliver too fair notice
Accosts to singlehood.
Tho lovely looks robe if turns drab,
Likely will style for sadden cheek blush.

I have trendy looks for axiom
Along attempts approach about
Upgrading singlehood.
Deck the sole garment
Till oft alone won't be altered
Till conceive of vary intellect
Till of what trend next you own.

Singleness is

stalking the only craft you do
till fetch the parts intrigue turns into.

Marriage is

dwelling beside one who will let you do
all the right projects you would have done
if not for one part you bound to one.

Dry yields exist for be watered.

## Mr. Harley Boone Likes

For him it's the train whistle stop
had added stoplight to the busy intersection.
And, too, bygones he younger added him stop
he around job went best.

He likes decade into satellite runs,
lovemaking and how runs fast the motor bike,
and babies don't cry every night.

And more his yen and yak the tale gets better
he tells of love for young and old.
Like he once met hot a spry skirt had his number
made who short of hair, his chats bold
no matter how he shook his chat would lumber.
I suspect, too, he had his drink or two talking.
But to him the achieving gets him to loving offer
how tenders checks life has to offer.
To him when more or less life serves you yet,
to him it comes to year by day gets how and what
more else to get!

## *Love Between Home Bodies*

To where can I run.
To whom can I turn
other than to mate should understand case to whom for the sum
I tell, don't lock arms around home all to know.
Yes, we live here with 3 natural born children who know all
too well we treasure them much like we treasure ourselves
the 2 of us. They even home schooled in this place.
Then, who else would I tell this our abode of little more we able
to do than bear with and group cater to each other.
Of else no other I'd ask
will our love continue along how it ranks rather
with seldom style designing for try outside to rather going after
what else and not for we destroy trust.
In the event we start to do something else uncover,
we have this opportunity. And should uncover discovery
of do what we love otherwise besides ourselves.

## If One This Best

If one this best for love could the heart not admire this
how fair, how real as only be true would be?
And how for keep bliss aflame on better hours gaiety must reign?
He breathes the chill in past urges flee
if the vice burns doubtful vice will add again fee.
What in to air advance how charming ways vent,
he has no need for man advance the inhumane charm then
he gets no kick of cramp the heart only sad.
If one this best for love award him this,
he's prone to outlast even summertime bliss.

## This Love Returns

You leave to only come back
with catching me by the arm,
walking whichever side you by.
At chill and sunshine legal hot and cool,
you never anchor your goodbyes.
There is no forever losing you.

## Ruminating In The Park

### Love in Days of Yore

It's a lovely day today
just like the day
a few decades ago
I first met my husband to be.
No rain nor gray tree seen,
only bright summer decked lace trendy at noon.
Near where the lot for wildflowers bloom,
there he smiled with delightedly there grab my hand.
I smiled back with delightedly take back my hand,
and quick steps I walked over the big bump in pavement
where the tweet tweet habit of birds.
Then was the first of many meetings were.
Later on, trend with dating nets love ripe insightfully enough
for man and gal become man and wife.
But why die so young?
is yet my sorrowful song.
I still miss how hugs and kisses grand.
Suddenly, too soon dead he was that suddenly gone
along with sidewalk cracks and bumps gone,
replaced by the modern run of a mobile run highway rode span.
Where sat amid the autumn bench in shade outlining turf,
I whispered, "Glad the old neighborhood gone,"
main to keep my tears for him in check.

If I could this park remake,
I would place the row of gladiola flowers
across the park grass is from corner to corner.
And pick one to take home and stand it up tall
where in glass vase main for arced on threshold the bloom would stand
simply as a token of love belongs reassuringly to
these memories arose of yore.

## Right in the Middle

He's right in there in the middle
of short except not all that
much short on call what you will
a talk or whim or chat.

He owns that right at midst of be
the middle age chap can do
but sit and chat illusion eve
with Jim and Mark and who.

Though more his wish in right on cue.
It matters woman in short skirt
be true than how mirages do;
imply she loves to flirt.

## Keeping it Going

As a child, I jumped at rope game the rebounding
"Keep the pot boiling"
sounds like what jovial duty mates do.
Only they keep the fire burning
that later in life for how burns for how rising
flame it pales light for stir it up again.

### Duty Requested With Love

There's a lot of what Love is for.
For mate, family, friends, money,
for teacher, school, science,
for trade, religion, sports, music,
plus arts and crafts, politics,
physical ed, hobbies, etcetera whatever.
And some like politics, for those who would be yet
still with learning how best service a request.

## A Love Profile

I'm like gone feasibly clear,
Clear as, now, serving shift in wet waves
The shift at ocean ledge waves appear.
And as they veer their seeming wet graves
Go through a tall transaction mirror,
I reel about some things.
They tilt themselves designing wet dance here
For splash dancing a due notice spring brings.
So, I am nervy churning twitches due
Like due the bride of earnest sighs linger
Should have her days reward more passion.
Yet, I am sound, baptized to love
Admires slick fowls of fashion
Squint far, cheat aberrance shift above
To know for part of me in love.

Leisure

Come into my leisure, main for visit.
Spring motive planted the notion people with
they trace at Love in the mix trails district.

# They Grow On Each Other

Spring though reprising cool breeze he knows
whose ginger tone
for times when her affection styles
main what he yes and no to.
And who made a short retreat in shawl and clads
no moan,
who back like in from chilly outside lawn.
She gets a man to feel announce past job hours
"I'm home"; and other times for he avoids to cater to,
she limits her distorted moan to bedroom do
for how regret a quieter bed
at even few the acts take long.
And this they relegate long hours to average rooms
the couch is rose and ceil's a stiff rock square till sounds
each calm endows who here with soundings tanager tunes
to spring maestro sounding him.
"Am I old for going bald this much?"
This answer in home it even housed an idle chair,
she merely said I am that much.
Words as uncalculated style implies he knows can't
mean all.
A fickle time she savors how turns on odd mix,
she turns on serves
she angles jester fuses craftiness with bliss.
All only serves he feels he knows his wife well.
And other feels he won't have,
she could tell when mate is in for this
he won't know he's in for, more chats his.

# The Way of Eilene

Her teats who nursed the babe beside
from cradle crib to breast;
her arms the warming embrace
as oft he loves he runs to best;
her lips to planted kisses
on wee for the arm scrapes
made the child would light behind;
her guise around pursuits
made the room in how pleasant climes;
her hurt, the rage her temperaments flame;
her looks the vain and clever laughs the same,
her love is how oft he runs home to,
to call to speak it long her name.
This is how he thinks of her deeds how esteemed
when he centers on Eilene.

## Designing More Than Love

There's a cast arranging under rays today,
cast it arranging cinders on the flowers.
And who designing words how gravely said,
a man to his wife he quotes how the hour.

There's a rustling makes each murmur heard
right for the wandering through meadow and hill.
Extreming beaks though multiplies kissing,
they have grave moments like mates must feel.

There's a wife deriving from this kind of quote
her mate designing, it gets on grave of reason
could more set her distraught heat on enlarge on reason.
Now, she of answer hot the heated passion
designing for an ending
to secret acts alike to treason
unless soon will his devotion seen.

## Accolades

A good one who care giver, truly is
a special diamond conducts chores where is
her loved ones will show they care
with choice hugs and kisses at times those arose
or spiced the compliments they rendered up.
It all says, "Thank you most for all you do."
Her tender affections for each of whom
she loves so dearly through her love shines true.
Her deeds like gems gleam, gleam for her own.
As for who works but another zone,
right hope is in receive some same respect
when you come home much to expect
a choice hug and a pat on the back. Yet in home from work
since you work hard, are your loved ones the clan
dutiful as help out with chores?
And, so, would clan so rather mop the floors no child for chores
battling what's on video games be?
Or be they more for double duty watch tv?
Working, you too deserve your amorous fee.
Whether hug or pat or radiant words.
Yes, you also resemble adored pearls.
Of course, one can't make husband of yours
go help out in the kitchen.
Award to mothers all or to most you are for truth
to family and friends a precious ruby.
May blessed your glad Mother Days!

## This Day I Love

This day I love,
And I'm in love
With summer allows
The long hours
Belong with city and yard
Ordinary fences guard
As the hours came alive and gave
To this decade
Ingredients given
To skill we live.

This day I love,
And I'm in love
With stay fertile trees
The racks in greenest leaves
Where people dwell today
Where dutiful of flight wings may
Between rack of tree stack stall.
Established men call—
This day we have,
Time past we had.

This day I love,
And I'm in love
With gaze beneath the sun
Looks on beloved everyone,

Too, who shrouded in gray cast
Engraves the spirit last.
Events we see today that are
Foreshadow events tomorrow.
This day I love,
And I'm in love with a mate
And with love true love.

Printed in the United States
By Bookmasters